posh®

Coloring
BOOK

· · · · · · · · · · · · · · ·

MANDALAS
FOR MEDITATION
& RELAXATION

Teresa Roberts Logan

· · · · · · · · · · · · · · ·

Andrews McMeel
Publishing®
a division of Andrews McMeel Universal

Dedicated to my dear, loving, hilarious father,
Gerald Greer Roberts, 1936–2016

Dad, 28, and me, 3

POSH® COLORING BOOK
MANDALAS FOR MEDITATION & RELAXATION

Andrews McMeel Publishing
a division of Andrews McMeel Universal
1130 Walnut Street, Kansas City, Missouri 64106

www.andrewsmcmeel.com

16 17 18 19 20 MLY 10 9 8 7 6 5 4 3 2 1

ISBN: 978-1-4494-8103-2

ATTENTION: SCHOOLS AND BUSINESSES
Andrews McMeel books are available at quantity discounts
with bulk purchase for educational, business, or sales
promotional use. For information, please e-mail the
Andrews McMeel Publishing Special Sales Department:
specialsales@amuniversal.com.

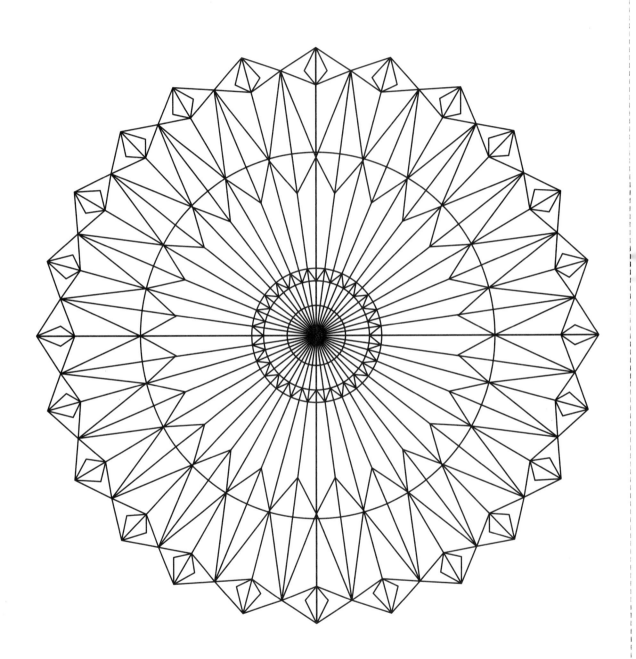

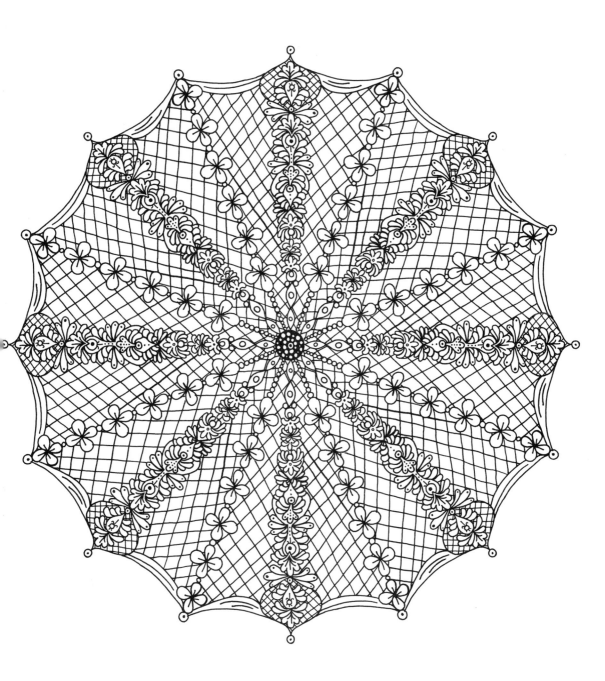

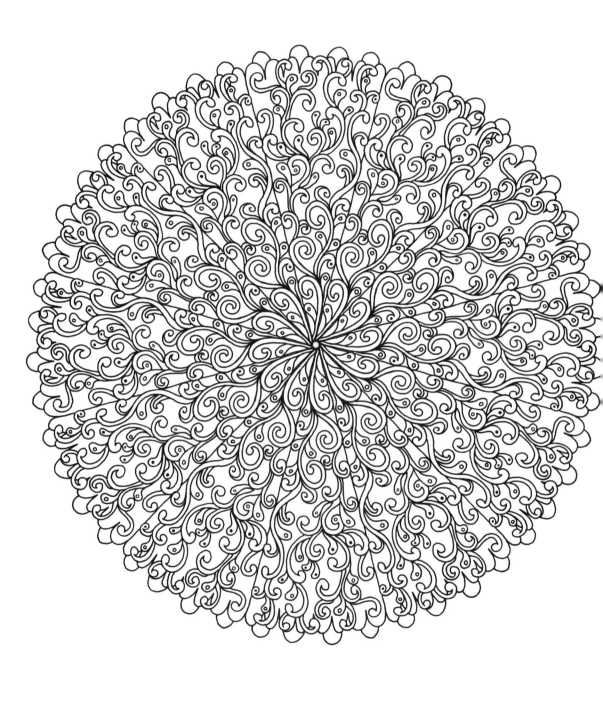